ANCIENT WORLDS

SURVIVING ANCIENT DROUGHTS, PLAGUES, AND NATURAL DISASTERS

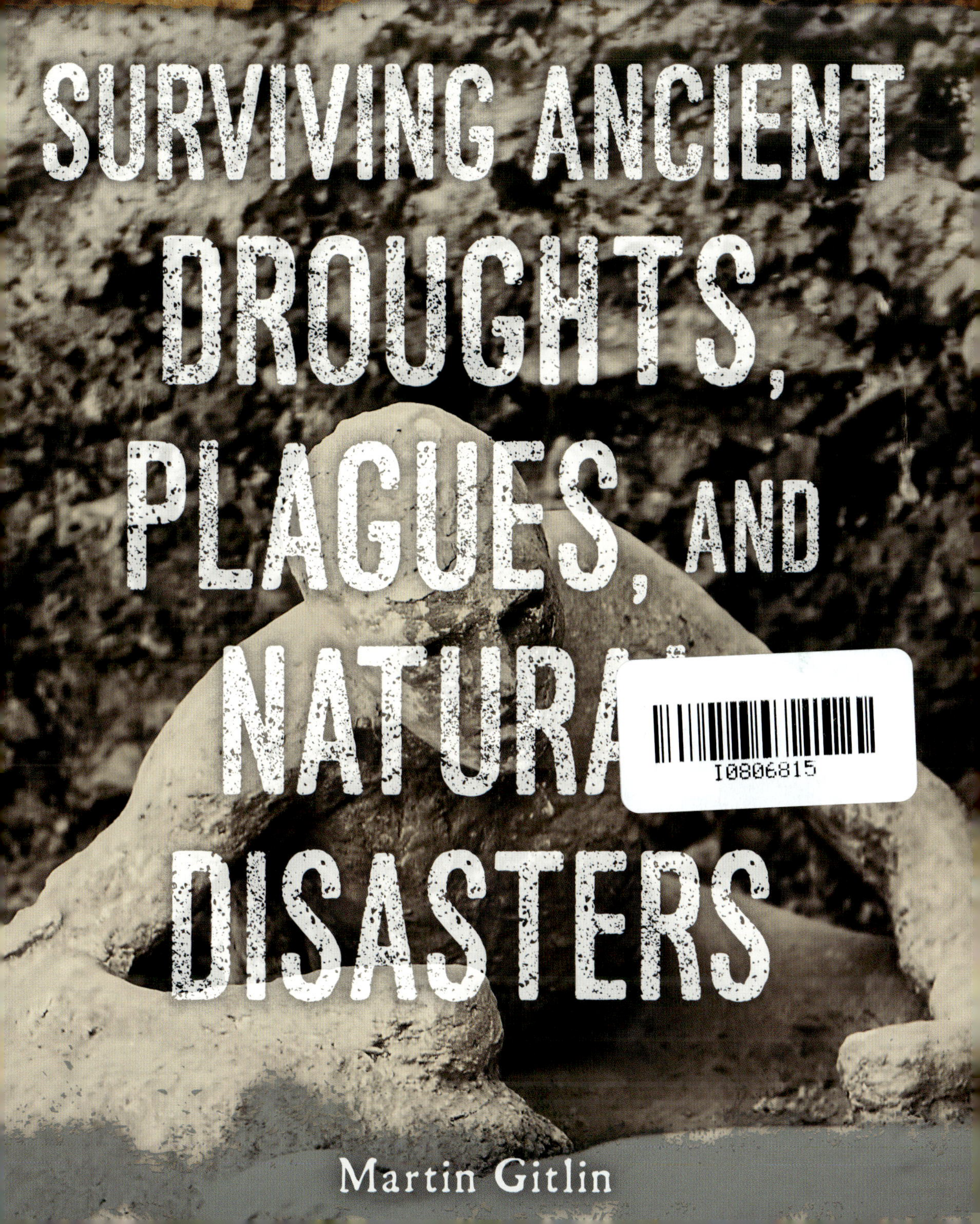

Martin Gitlin

45TH PARALLEL PRESS

Published in the United States of America by Cherry Lake Publishing Group
Ann Arbor, Michigan
www.cherrylakepublishing.com

Reading Adviser: Beth Walker Gambro, MS, Ed., Reading Consultant, Yorkville, IL

Photo Credits: © BlackMac /Shutterstock, cover, title page; © imagedepotpro/iStock.com, 4; © panitanphoto/Shutterstock, 7; © Renata Sedmakova/Shutterstock, 8; © Anastasios71/Shutterstock, 10; Walter Crane, Public domain, via Wikimedia Commons, 12; © Vihang Ghalsasi/Shutterstock, 15; © Stasia04/Shutterstock, 16; © giedrius_b/Shutterstock, 18; © Christian Delbert/Shutterstock, 20; © Fer Gregory/Shutterstock, 23; © Alexandree/Shutterstock, 24; Karl Bryullov, Public domain, via Wikimedia Commons, 26; © Yasemin Olgunoz Berber/Shutterstock, 28; © Only Fabrizio/Shutterstock, 30

Graphic Element Credits: Graphic Element Credits: Cover, multiple interior pages: © Andrey_Kuzmin/Shutterstock, © cajoer/Shutterstock, © GUSAK OLENA/Shutterstock, © Eky Studio/Shutterstock

45TH Parallel Press is an imprint of Cherry Lake Publishing Group.

Library of Congress Cataloging-in-Publication Data has been filed and is available at catalog.loc.gov.

Cherry Lake Publishing Group would like to acknowledge the work of the Partnership for 21st Century Learning, a Network of Battelle for Kids. Please visit http://www.battelleforkids.org/networks/p21 for more information.

Printed in the United States of America

Note from publisher: Websites change regularly, and their future contents are outside of our control. Supervise children when conducting any recommended online searches for extended learning opportunities.

About the Author
Martin Gitlin is an educational book author based in Connecticut. He won more than 45 awards as a newspaper journalist from 1991 to 2002. Included was a first-place award from the Associated Press. That organization voted him as one of the top four feature writers in Ohio in 2002. Martin has had about 250 books published since 2006. Most of them were written for students. He has authored many books about history.

TABLE OF CONTENTS

INTRODUCTION

The world population has grown. It went from 4 million to 8 billion. This happened over the last 12,000 years.

Imagine ancient people in modern times. They'd be stunned. They'd see jets. They'd see tall buildings. They'd be confused by computers.

Some things haven't changed. Humans still deal with natural disasters. Examples are wildfires and floods. Sickness continues to take lives. **Plagues** remain a threat. Plagues are sicknesses that spread. They're deadly. COVID-19 is one example.

There are differences. People today know more. Science has given us medicines. Medicines cure sicknesses. We can predict weather. We know where and when storms will strike. We have tools to fix damages. People live longer lives. They have easier lives.

Ancient people faced more dangers. Plagues were deadlier then. They wiped out millions. Cures didn't exist. Ancient people relied on natural treatments.

Ancient people also experienced natural disasters. But they were surprised. Earthquakes leveled towns. Volcanoes burned homes. They burned people. Droughts destroyed farms. Crops failed. The result was **famine**. Famines are food shortages. People starved to death.

Today, these things still happen. But scientists can warn us. After, people can help more. People send aid. They send food. They send water. They send trucks and planes.

Ancient people could do little. They could only bury their dead. They rebuilt homes. They started over. They tried to improve their lives. They did whatever they could. That need to survive? All people have that.

Hunger remains a big problem today. About 800 million people are underfed.

CHAPTER ONE

Modern-day Thera is Santorini. Today, Santorini has just 15,000 residents. But the island has 2 million visitors per year.

The Minoan Eruption

Minoa had many port cities in ancient Greece. It was around 1645 BCE. The Minoans were thriving. They lived on the island of Thera. They had big homes. Their homes had 2 floors. The rooms were nicely decorated. The Minoans owned beautiful pottery. Everything seemed well.

Then it was gone. All the homes were burned. No human remains were found. Some believe the Minoans knew what was coming. So they fled. But the volcano destroyed all they had.

It began with a volcano. It erupted. Boiling hot **magma** poured out. Magma is hot, melted rock. Then, the volcano collapsed. This happened many times. But the Minoan eruption was the biggest. Thera was not safe.

The eruption wrecked the Minoan world. It was one of the worst eruptions in human history. It was even felt in China. Ancient Chinese texts noted "a yellow fog." Ashes from the volcano blocked the sun.

The eruption destroyed the area. It caused earthquakes. It caused **tsunamis**. Tsunamis are big sea waves. The islands were changed. They were covered with rock. All life was killed.

There were no personal accounts. Scientists studied the disaster. Ash deposits were found. They were on the ocean floor.

Plato was a Greek philosopher. He described the lost city of Atlantis. He did this around 360 BCE. He might have been referring to the Thera volcano.

A NICE STORY

Modern people joke about ancient medical care. There is truth to those stories. Many illnesses had no working treatments. The science of medicine was new. But the ancient Egyptians had answers. They used natural cures. Some are still used today.

One is honey. It helps with swelling. The Egyptians rubbed it on wounds. The British military used honey to treat burns. Another is willow trees and shrubs. Willow treated toothaches. Its bark inspired aspirin.

Egyptians also used mint. Mint eased stomach pain. That is another cure that remains popular. The same is true of pomegranate. That is a fruit. Egyptians ate it to treat parasitic worms. They were known then as snakes in the stomach. Pomegranates stopped these worms. Parasites feed off their host.

CHAPTER TWO

In Greek and Roman legend, King Midas was a famous king of Phrygia. Phrygia is part of modern-day Turkey. Myth claims everything Midas touched turned to gold.

Disastrous Droughts

The Bronze Age was an era. This era existed for 2,000 years. Hundreds of **civilizations** thrived. Civilizations are human societies. They were in Europe. They were in Asia. They were in Africa. Some were stronger than others.

Among them were the Hittites. They lived in what is now Turkey. Their empire reached modern-day Syria and Iraq. The Hittites ruled for 500 years. Their military was as strong as that of Egypt.

What destroyed the Hittites? It was a severe **drought**. Droughts are dry periods. Little or no rain fell for 3 years. That caused crop failures. It caused famine. Hittite leaders couldn't handle it. The empire fell.

Modern India has 1.4 billion people. Pakistan has 250 million. There were far fewer in ancient times. But both countries were thriving.

One was the Harappans. They existed between 3300 and 1300 BCE. Their cities had about 50,000 people. The Harappans were advanced. They built complex **sewage** systems. Sewage is wastewater. They relied on flooding of the Indus River. That helped **irrigate** their crops. Irrigate means to water lands. The Harappans built wells. They made drains. They made dams. That controlled water flow.

But they couldn't control droughts. Summer **monsoons** decreased around 2500 BCE. Monsoons are storms. Less monsoons meant more droughts. So people moved to the mountains. They expected more rainfall there. But that land dried up too. A once great civilization was gone. Droughts wiped out the Harappans.

These are Harappan ruins in India. Scientists studied the drought that affected the Harappans. They think it was caused by a lack of monsoons.

CHAPTER THREE

Spartans weren't as affected by the plagues in Athens. But they still didn't win victory over Athens.

Perilous Plagues

Smallpox is a sickness. It was **eradicated** by 1980. Eradicate means to get rid of. Typhus is another sickness. It's no longer a killer. But both were common in ancient Athens. People had rashes. They had fevers. Age or gender didn't matter. Neither did wealth. Nobody was spared. Many didn't survive.

It was 430 BCE. Smallpox and typhus plagues hit Athens hard. Most in Athens were infected. Deaths were high. Over 100,000 died. That's about 25 percent of the people.

Athens was also attacked by Sparta. Sparta was a warrior society. It's also in Greece. The attacking Spartans weren't as affected. But it didn't help Sparta win. The war ended in 404 BCE. That was 20 years after the plagues.

One man shared his story. He was Thucydides. He was a Greek historian. He described the horror. He did it for future people. He knew sickness could hit again. His story helped people cure those diseases. His writings helped doctors. They helped researchers.

Thucydides gave many details. He explained how the plague attacked. He noted bloody throats. He noted bloody tongues. He wrote about hard coughs. He wrote about vomiting. He described violent **spasms**. Spasms are muscle twitches. People felt intense heat. They felt their insides burning. Victims were dead within 9 days.

Those who cared for the sick in ancient times often caught the same sicknesses. They died soon after their patients.

MYSTERY SOLVED OR UNSOLVED?

Emperor Yao was the ruler of China in 2500 BCE. That year, there was the Great Flood of Gun-Yu. Not much is known. Much has been claimed. One is that it lasted 20 years. Another is that it forced a great migration. Migration is the moving from one place to another. Many left their homes. They moved to high hills or mountains. Some even nested in trees.

There is some proof of a flood. It happened along the Yellow River. It happened around 1920 BCE. But that date does not fit the myth. The story says Yao asked his advisors how to control the flood. The advisors were known as the Four Mountains. They told Yao to use his cousin Gun. Gun failed to stop the rushing waters. So did others. It was finally done by Yu. Yu was the son of co-emperor Shun. Yu did the logical thing. He built drainage systems. Is that story true? Nobody knows.

CHAPTER FOUR

Ancient Mayan civilization had advanced technology for the time. Their systems helped them survive drought.

Mayans Fight Drought

Drought remains a world problem. A lack of rainfall is deadly. There isn't enough drinking water. Crops don't grow. People can't find food. They often starve. Dust blows around from the dry ground. The dust causes sicknesses. It harms lungs. It harms eyes.

Did ancient peoples survive drought? The ancient Mayans did. The ancient Mayans lived in Central America. Their area was around southern Mexico. It was warm there.

The ancient Mayans had solutions. They built systems to fight drought. This is why they lasted around 3,000 years.

The ancient Mayans built a dam. It was in the city of Tikal. There were no bulldozers then. They built it by hand. It was a big job. The ancient Mayans cut stone. They used rubble. They used dirt. This worked. The dam was 260 feet (79 meters) long. It was 33 feet (10 m) high. It held 20 million gallons (76 million liters) of water.

The ancient Mayans weren't done. They didn't rely on rain falling into the dam. They built paved surfaces with canals. That water fed into large water bins. They added a water cleaning system. They placed sandboxes in the canals. That filtered water.

Drought was deadly to ancient people. But not the ancient Mayans. They defeated drought.

Spanish conquerors arrived in the 1500s. They brought sickness and war. This ended the ancient Mayan civilization.

CHAPTER FIVE

Pompeii still exists. It's under Mount Vesuvius. This mountain last erupted in 1944.

The Vesuvius Volcano

It was 79 CE. The Roman Empire was born 110 years earlier. Pompeii was prosperous. The city had 12,000 to 20,000 people. Many were farmers. Many others sold goods. Vineyards and orchards flourished. Herculaneum was a nearby town. It was also doing fine. Rich Romans visited in the summer. They spent lots of money.

Both cities were at the base of Mount Vesuvius. That was at the Bay of Naples. Nobody was worried. Vesuvius hadn't erupted for 1,800 years.

Then it happened. It was October. The peak of Vesuvius exploded. Hot ash and **pumice** spread. Pumice is hard lava. The ash and pumice spread 10 miles (16 kilometers) wide. It rained down on Pompeii.

People ran in fear. Some stayed inside. They hoped to wait out the eruption. The destruction soon reached Herculaneum. A cloud of hot ash took over the cities. It burned all who remained. Volcanic mud buried Herculaneum. The people of Pompeii **suffocated**. This means they couldn't breathe. Homes fell. Those who stayed were buried alive.

Pliny the Younger wrote about the eruption. He was 17 years old. He was staying near the Bay of Naples. He wrote that people covered their heads with pillows. It was their only defense. Others prayed to die. Pliny the Younger escaped. But his uncle didn't. His uncle was Pliny the Elder.

Pliny the Elder commanded a Roman fleet. He sent it to Pompeii. He wanted to help volcano victims. He was killed by toxic gas.

ANCIENT RULES

Burying the dead was sacred to the ancient Greeks. Not doing so was insulting. It offended the dead. It also offended the gods. The Greeks believed burials helped the soul of the dead rest. Anyone finding a dead body had to at least throw dirt over it. Not doing so was illegal. That was true in war. Greek law even required respecting dead enemy soldiers.

Ancient Athens had strict burial rules. The eyes of the dead were closed. A coin was put in the mouth. The coin was called an obol. That was passage money for Charon. Charon was a mythical figure. He transported the dead. He took them to the world beyond. The dead body was washed. It was dressed in white clothing. It was decorated with ivy garlands. Garlands are strings of flowers. The body was placed on a couch. The face was turned toward the door. Friends and relatives mourned. It was illegal to show fake grief. Sometimes women were hired to sing. Sometimes there was a flute player.

CHAPTER SIX

Pieces of Ancient Antioch remain. The Vespasianus Titus Tunnel was built as a water tunnel for the port of Antioch.

Earthquake in Antioch

Antioch was a city in ancient Syria. It was part of the Roman Empire. It had a forum. It had a theater. It featured public baths. An **aqueduct** carried water to homes. Aqueducts are systems that transport water. It was known as a fun-loving place. All was well until 115 CE.

An earthquake struck. It impacted over 500,000 people. It also killed many visitors. The city was destroyed. So were nearby towns.

Cassius Dio was a Roman historian. He shared details. The earthquake began with a roar. Then came quaking. Buildings leaped into the air. They broke into pieces. The ground opened. The wreckage began. Falling buildings crushed people. About 260,000 were killed.

Antioch was rebuilt. A new aqueduct was built. So was a theater. Many people had survived. So had Antioch.

Centuries passed. It was 526 CE. The 115 CE quake was in the past. Homes and buildings were built stronger. Nobody expected disaster. Antioch was crowded that day. Visitors arrived to celebrate a holiday.

John Malalas was an Antioch writer. He explained what happened next. There was another earthquake. The ground began to boil. Buildings caught fire. So did the people running from them. The city was destroyed. Malalas said 250,000 people died.

There were "Five Good Emperors of Rome." They ruled during a prosperous period. Trajan and Hadrian were among them. Emperor Trajan is shown here.

VERY IMPORTANT PEOPLE

Titus was a Roman emperor. He ruled for 3 years. His reign was short. But it was eventful. He dealt with 2 big disasters. And he did it with kindness.

The first was the Vesuvius eruption. That happened only a few months after his rule began. It nearly destroyed the Bay of Naples. Pompeii and Herculaneum were buried. Thousands died. Titus appointed 2 experts. His team organized relief efforts. Titus used money from the Roman reserves to aid victims. Reserves are savings. Titus even visited Pompeii twice to help.

Another disaster followed. That was a fire in Rome. It burned large parts of the city. The blaze lasted 3 days and nights. Buildings were destroyed. Included were the Pantheon and the Temple of Jupiter. The Theater of Pompey was also badly damaged. Titus again gave money for the relief effort.

GLOSSARY

aqueduct (AH-kwuh-dukt) a structure that carries flowing water

civilizations (sih-vuh-luh-ZAY-shunz) the cultures of particular times or places

drought (DROWT) a long period of low rainfall and dry weather conditions

eradicated (ih-RA-duh-kayt-id) eliminated completely

famine (FA-muhn) the lack of food affecting people in a wide area

irrigate (EER-uh-gayt) to supply crops with water

magma (MAG-muh) molten rock within Earth released when a volcano erupts; called lava when it reaches Earth's surface

monsoons (mahn-SOONZ) wind systems of the Indian Ocean that bring heavy rain

plagues (PLAYGZ) wide-spreading sicknesses that cause high death rates

pumice (PUH-muhs) hardened lava

sewage (SOO-ij) wastewater and waste matter carried off by sewers

spasms (SPA-zuhmz) sudden, uncontrolled muscle contractions

suffocated (SUH-fuh-kayt-id) died because of lack of air

tsunamis (SOO-nah-meez) huge sea waves often caused by an earthquake or volcano

LEARN MORE

Baby Professor. *What Happened to Pompeii? Ancient Rome History for Kids*. Baby Professor, 2017.

Fullman, Joseph. *Ancient Civilizations: Discover the Golden Ages of History, from Ancient Egypt and Greece through Mighty Rome and the Maya*. New York: DK Children, 2013.

Search online with an adult:
Ancient History for Kids: Ancient China

INDEX